Novels for Students, Volume 8

Staff

Series Editor: Deborah A. Stanley.

Contributing Editors: Peg Bessette, Sara L. Constantakis, Catherine L. Goldstein, Dwayne D. Hayes, Motoko Fujishiro Huthwaite, Arlene M. Johnson, Angela Yvonne Jones, James E. Person, Jr., Polly Rapp, Erin White.

Editorial Technical Specialist: Tim White.

Managing Editor: Joyce Nakamura.

Research: Victoria B. Cariappa, *Research Team Manager*. Andy Malonis, *Research Specialist*. Tamara C. Nott, Tracie A. Richardson, and Cheryl L. Warnock, *Research Associates*. Jeffrey Daniels, *Research Assistant*.

Permissions: Susan M. Trosky, *Permissions Manager*. Maria L. Franklin, *Permissions Specialist*. Sarah Tomacek, *Permissions Associate*.

Production: Mary Beth Trimper, *Production Director*. Evi Seoud, *Assistant Production Manager*. Cindy Range, *Production Assistant*.

Graphic Services: Randy Bassett, *Image Database Supervisor*. Robert Duncan and Michael Logusz, *Imaging Specialists*. Pamela A. Reed, *Photography Coordinator*. Gary Leach, *Macintosh Artist*.

Product Design: Cynthia Baldwin, *Product Design Manager*. Cover Design: Michelle DiMercurio, *Art Director*. Page Design: Pamela A. E. Galbreath, *Senior Art Director*.

Copyright Notice

Since this page cannot legibly accommodate all copyright notices, the acknowledgments constitute an extension of the copyright notice.

While every effort has been made to secure permission to reprint material and to ensure the reliability of the information presented in this publication, Gale Research neither guarantees the accuracy of the data contained herein nor assumes any responsibility for errors, omissions, or discrepancies. Gale accepts no payment for listing; and inclusion in the publication of any organization, agency, institution, publication, service, or individual does not imply endorsement of the editors or publisher. Errors brought to the attention of the publisher and verified to the satisfaction of the publisher will be corrected in future editions.

This publication is a creative work fully protected by all applicable copyright laws, as well as by misappropriation, trade secret, unfair competition, and other applicable laws. The authors and editors of this work have added value to the underlying factual material herein through one or more of the following: unique and original selection, coordination, expression, arrangement, and classification of the information. All rights to this publication will be vigorously defended.

Copyright © 2000
The Gale Group
27500 Drake Rd.
Farmington Hills, MI 48331-3535

All rights reserved including the right of reproduction in whole or in part in any form.

ISBN 0-7876-3827-7
ISSN 1094-3552

Printed in the United States of America.
10 9 8 7 6 5 4 3 2 1

The Old Gringo

Carlos Fuentes 1985

Introduction

The Old Gringo is one of Carlos Fuentes's best-known works. It is a complex novel that intertwines psychology, mythology, and political events to examine the culture of modern Mexico. At the core of the story is the disappearance of Ambrose Bierce, an American newspaperman and short-story writer. Bierce, who is most remembered for his brutally sardonic parody *The Devil's Dictionary* and the often-anthologized short story "An Occurrence at Owl Creek Bridge," left his job and home in 1913 at age seventy-one and disappeared, never to be heard from again. Speculation has held that he went to

Mexico to join Pancho Villa in fighting the revolution, but there has never been conclusive evidence to support this. Bierce is the old gringo referred to in this novel's title. The story focuses on the relationships the character forms in Mexico with Harriet Winslow, a schoolteacher from Washington, DC, and with General Tomás Arroyo, leader of the revolutionary band that is on its way to meet up with Villa's army. The three form a triangle, exploring questions of love, respect, and sensuality in ways that highlight the differences between Mexican and American ways of thinking. A few years after the book was published, it was adapted into a motion picture starring Jane Fonda, Jimmy Smits, and Gregory Peck as the old gringo.

Author Biography

Carlos Fuentes is considered one of the preeminent voices in Mexican literature in the last half of the twentieth century. He was born in Panama City, Panama, in 1928, and is the son of a Mexican diplomat. Throughout his childhood, he moved from one country to another, living in Chile, Argentina, and the United States. In his early years, he spent much time in Washington, DC, which is described vividly in *The Old Gringo*. He attended high school in Mexico City and received degrees from the National University of Mexico and the Institut des Hautes-Etudes in Geneva, Switzerland.

Fuentes's writing career developed after he already had a successful career in the diplomatic corps. Even after he was an internationally recognized novelist, he remained in politics, holding such positions as the chief of the Department of Cultural Relations of Mexico's Ministry of Foreign Affairs, and, from 1975 to 1977, as his country's ambassador to France. His development as a writer coincided with the emergence of a Latin American avante garde during the late 1950s and early 1960s. This movement also included Julio Cortazar and Nobel laureate Gabriel García Márquez.

Fuentes's fiction has developed throughout the years. His first novels, *The Good Conscience* and *Where the Air Is Clear*, reflect the author's concern with Mexican identity, using the magical realism techniques that came to be associated with him and his peers. Fuentes's prose is so richly luxurious that readers find it hard to distinguish between actions that are presented as reality and those that are the dreams or fantasies of the characters. The same features have appeared in Fuentes's later books, but over the years his novels have become less rooted in the imagination and increasingly more representative of reality. Fuentes has also written extensively about politics, exploring Mexico and Latin America's place in the world culture as well as his country's identity in relation to the United States. Since the publication of *The Old Gringo* in 1985, his nonfiction writings have vastly outnumbered his fictional works. Fuentes's most recent novel is 1995's *Diana, The Goddess Who Hunts Alone*, which was based on his affair in the 1960s with the actress Jean Seeberg.

Plot Summary

The Old Lady Remembers

Though the protagonist of *The Old Gringo* is Ambrose Bierce, and the novel an extended meditation on his possible fate, Bierce's name is not mentioned until the final pages of the book. The novel takes place within the frame narrative—an old lady remembering. Bracketed by her act of memory, the story of Tomás Arroyo, Harriet Winslow, and the old gringo is pieced together in a dizzying series of multi-layered perspectives, voices, and times. It starts with the gringo's corpse being disinterred so it can be sent back to the United States. As they uncover his desiccated body, the diggers share their memories of him. He had come to Mexico to die, and no one ever found out who he was.

The Old Gringo Arrives

With the railway bridge burning behind him, the old gringo buys a horse at El Paso and rides off across the border into the deserts of Mexico. He is looking for Pancho Villa and the revolution. He is looking for death. The narrative shifts to the perspective of the revolutionaries, watching him approach. They immediately understand that he has a death wish. Introduced to the General, Tomás Arroyo, the gringo offers his services as a fighter, and is mocked until he proves his marksmanship by shooting a tossed peso through the center. Pedro—then a boy, later one of the voices that remembers the gringo as his body is dug up—is given the peso. Arroyo agrees to let the old gringo stay.

General Tomás Arroyo

The gringo rides with Arroyo in a lavish train carriage—plunder from the revolution. On their way to the Miranda Hacienda, Arroyo's current base and his past home, the general explains the nature of Mexican history and his right to reclaim the Mirandas' property. He carries with him a set of ancient papers, sealed by the King of Spain, that granted perpetual land rights to his people. As he explains, he cannot read, so the papers act as an icon that validates and represents his hereditary memory. As they arrive at the hacienda, it is burning to the ground.

Harriet Winslow

The hacienda is decorated with hanged bodies and jubilant crowds. The only thing left standing is the mirrored ballroom, and in a thematically vital moment, the peasants gaze at their reflections, realizing for the first time that they are whole, physical individuals. In the midst of the mayhem is Harriet Winslow—a prim, responsible spinster from Washington, DC, who had been hired by the Mirandas as a governess. Her Protestant work ethic, she says, compels her to stay and finish the job for which she has been paid—"improving" children. Through a series of flashbacks and conversations with the old gringo, we learn that she is genteelly impoverished—she and her mother have lived on a military pension after her father disappeared during the action in Cuba.

The First Campaign

The old gringo and Harriet have begun to enter each other's dreams. The troops ride off to fight the Federales, and the gringo leads the decoy charge across the plains. As the gringo rides out, he is lost in a version of one of his most famous stories, a tale of patricide in the U.S. Civil War, and this image of a son killing a father is reworked as a symbol of revolution throughout the novel. Hailed as a hero, he returns to the hacienda, which Harriet has been ordering the peasants to rebuild. Undermining her unwillingness to comprehend, a series of voices from the past and present explain the reasons for the revolution to her. She and the gringo drink together, and she learns his identity, but does not name him. She understands that he has rejected that name in favor of the generic term "gringo."

The Federales

During the second engagement, Arroyo's troops take many prisoners. Those who refuse to join the cause will be killed, and Arroyo demands that the old gringo be the one who shoots them. Arroyo says that a man as brave as the gringo is dangerous, and must prove his loyalty. The gringo deliberately misses the captain of the opposing troops, and Arroyo kills him instead. As they ride back, the gringo realizes that though he came here to die, he has rediscovered life, fear, and his need to write. Back at the hacienda, Harriet has spent the day exhorting the revolutionaries to establish a new society, and trying to teach them "Christian virtues." When a string of pearls goes missing, she dismisses the revolutionaries as larcenous. Later, Arroyo will show her that the necklace has been taken to the chapel and placed on a statue of the Virgin Mary. Harriet knows herself to be alien, and has uneasy dreams in which Mexican voices speak to her, and her father's death is revealed as something other than what she had said.

Tomás and Harriet

Arroyo and Harriet make love in the mirrored ballroom, and Harriet knows that she is experiencing life and love for the first time. As she said in the first pages of the novel, she will always hate Arroyo for showing her what she could never be. Afterwards, he explains his relationship to the hacienda. He grew up there as a servant. She tells the old gringo what happened, and says that she did it to protect the gringo from Arroyo. The gringo tells her he loves her, but it's too late—she and Arroyo are like his children to him now. Harriet reveals that her father didn't die at all, but stayed in Cuba to live with "a negress." Now that Harriet has experienced physical love, she understands her father better.

The Old Gringo Dies

Arroyo returns. The old gringo goes into the train car, and Arroyo follows him. Shots are fired, and the gringo stumbles out, Arroyo following and shooting. The gringo is holding Arroyo's talismanic papers—they are burning. The gringo dies facedown in the dirt, and the burnt words send echoes through the desert. Now another story begins. The narrative switches to a point later in time, where Pancho Villa is being interviewed by the U.S. press. They ask him about a U.S. citizen murdered by Arroyo and buried in the desert. Harriet Winslow has claimed that the old gringo is her father, and is demanding the return of his body.

The End—The Death of General Arroyo

The exhumation of the old gringo's body is juxtaposed with Arroyo's final conversation with Harriet. While the corpse is dug up and shot in the front for the sake of military etiquette, we learn that Arroyo was a Miranda—the son of the hacienda owner. Shocked, Harriet accuses him of being merely a disgruntled heir. Back at the grave, Villa asks Arroyo to deliver the coup de grace to the gringo's body. As he does so, Villa's troops open fire. Arroyo dies shouting "Viva Villa!" The gringo's corpse is buried in Arlington Cemetery. In the final pages, Harriet says his name—Ambrose Bierce—and returns to the point at which the novel began: "Now she sits alone and remembers."

Characters

Doroteo Arango

See Pancho Villa

Tomás Arroyo

Tomás Arroyo is the general of the revolutionaries. The plan is supposed to be that Arroyo will lead his band of soldiers across the northern state of Mexico and meet up with the forces of Pancho Villa later to attack Mexico City. In reality, though, Arroyo is hesitant to leave his encampment at the Miranda hacienda. The Mirandas were a wealthy family, "owners of half the state of Chihuahua and parts of Durango and Coahuila as well." Arroyo is the illegitimate result of a union between the head of the Miranda family and one of the servants, and though he was raised on the estate, he has never been recognized as a relative. Now that the revolution has driven the Mirandas out, Arroyo seems to relish his position as master of the household, and he hesitates leading his troops' departure.

Arroyo has a box of documents in his possession that was given to him by another servant on the estate, Graciano, an old man who died soon after turning the papers over. Arroyo explains that the ancient documents grant the land to his people, by order of the King of Spain, but as Bierce points out, Arroyo is illiterate and does not really know what is written on the papers.

Arroyo develops an intimate relationship with Harriet on the night that the revolutionaries are celebrating a victory over the federal forces, a victory due in large part to Bierce's reckless bravery. In part, Arroyo wants her because she is someone to whom he can explain his people's struggle, as well as someone cultured and sophisticated who can recognize him for more than a greedy criminal. However, his actions toward Harriet are also motivated by jealousy for the admiration that she shows Bierce.

When Bierce destroys the documents toward which Arroyo had been so reverent, Arroyo kills him in frustration. Harriet, angry with him, shouts out, "You poor bastard. You are Tomás Miranda," humiliating him by implying that he has the same values as his landowning father. After having the corpse of the old gringo executed "properly," Pancho Villa tricks Arroyo into standing near the gringo's body against the wall: "Give him the coup de grace," he tells Arroyo, "you know you're like a son to me. Do it well. We have to do everything aboveboard and according to the law. This time I don't want you to make me any mistakes." He then gives the firing squad the order to shoot Arroyo, and fires the final, lethal bullet into Arroyo himself.

Ambrose Bierce

Part of the story of the old gringo—his death—is based on the fate of William Benton, a British citizen who was beaten to death by Pancho Villa's men, and whose body was later dug up, formally executed, and sent home. The rest of the gringo's story is based on what is known about the last days of the writer Ambrose Bierce. Most of the details given about the character in the book fit with the facts of Bierce's life: he was a satirist, short-story writer, and journalist, who lived in San Francisco for much of his life and wrote for the newspaper chain owned by William Randolph Hearst. In 1913, at the age of seventy-one, Bierce left everything he had and went to Mexico to join Pancho Villa and his band. There is no historical record of what happened to Bierce after he crossed the border, and this is where the novel picks up his story.

A well-known cynic, the old gringo is tired of the hypocrisy of American life, and of life in general: he describes himself to Harriet Winslow as "[a] contemptible muckraking reporter at the service of a baron of the press as corrupt as any I denounce in his name. I attack the honor and dishonor of all men, without distinction. In my time, I was feared and hated." Having traveled to Mexico to die in the revolution, Bierce has the advantage of not fearing death in battle. This attitude earns him the admiration of the revolutionary band he joins after he rides straight into the enemy's gunfire.

The old gringo's relationship with the schoolteacher Harriet Winslow, however, gives him something for which to live. His relationship with

Harriet is complex. To a certain degree they are lovers: the narrator explains that she gives him, not Arroyo, the right to dream about her. However, their relationship never becomes a physical one, like the relationship Harriet has with Arroyo. To both Harriet and Arroyo, Bierce is a father figure, replacing the fathers that rejected them both in childhood. The old gringo, however, is later killed by Arroyo after the gringo burns Arroyo's precious papers.

Frutos Garcia

Frutos Garcia is a colonel in the revolutionary army; he is one of the people responsible for digging up the old gringo's body in the opening scene. He appears periodically throughout the novel, expressing opinions about the actions of the three main characters and explaining Mexican customs to Harriet. At a certain point, Harriet recalls that it was Colonel Garcia who gave the order to kill his friend Mansalvo after Mansalvo was caught stealing gold coins from a derailed train car in Charco Blanco.

La Garduña

La Garduña joined the revolution from a house of prostitution in Durango. She plans to be buried in holy ground when she dies; her family is going to tell the priest that she is her virginal Aunt Josefa. Harriet saves La Garduña's two-year-old child from choking by sucking the phlegm out of her mouth and earns La Garduña's gratitude.

Graciano

An old man on the Miranda hacienda while Arroyo was growing up, Graciano was responsible for winding all of the clocks, and so was entrusted with keys to all of the rooms. When he took young Tomás Arroyo with him on his rounds one day, and let the boy carry his key ring, the master of the house severely admonished him. Graciano taught the boy about dignity and refusing charity. Before he died, he gave the box of ancient papers with the seal of the King of Spain to young Arroyo to watch over.

La Luna

La Luna is one of Arroyo's lovers. She met him when he hid in the basement of her house in a small town in Durango. Her husband was a moneylender, and when the revolutionaries came through town they took him out to the corral and shot him. Arroyo was trapped in the basement when Federal troops came chasing the revolutionaries—the moneylender had nailed boards over the basement door. La Luna pulled the boards up after the troops left, saving Arroyo's life.

Inocencio Mansalvo

Inocencio Mansalvo is a Mexican peasant who is traveling with the revolutionary band. He was a peasant field-worker before he joined them. At the end, after the death of Arroyo and Bierce, it is Mansalvo who is responsible for escorting Harriet back to the American border. There, she takes her first good look at him: "He was a thin man, with green eyes and hair black as an Oriental's; two deep clefts furrowed his cheeks, two marked the corners of his mouth, and two crossed his forehead, all in pairs, as if twin artisans had hurriedly hacked him out with a machete, the sooner to thrust him out in the world…. Until this minute, she had never *looked* at this man." In her last moments with Mansalvo, Harriet comes to understand the Mexican people better.

Old Gringo

See Ambrose Bierce

Pedrito

See Pedro

Pedro

Pedro is the eleven-year-old boy who first talks to Bierce and leads him into the camp of the revolutionaries. He gains respect for Bierce when the old man shoots a peso in the air, and Arroyo lets Pedro keep the peso as a souvenir. Pedro's last words to the old gringo's corpse as it is shipped across the border are, "The way you wanted it, old man. Pancho Villa himself gave you the coup de grace."

Media Adaptations

- *The Old Gringo* was adapted for film and released by Columbia Pictures in 1989. The motion picture was directed by Luis Puenzo and starred Gregory Peck, Jane Fonda, and Jimmy Smits.

- The video titled *Carlos Fuentes* was released by Ediciones del Norte and Television Productions and Services Inc. in 1983.

- *Carlos Fuentes: Bridging the 20th and 21st Centuries*, another video, was released by Metropolitan State College in 1998.

- *Bill Moyers' A World of Ideas, Volume 8: Carlos Fuentes* was released on video by Films for the Humanities in 1994.

- *Carlos Fuentes: A Video* was released by Lannan Foundation in 1989.
- The video *Carlos Fuentes: A Man of Two Worlds* was released by A. J. Casciero in 1988.
- *Crossing Borders: The Journey of Carlos Fuentes* was released on video by Home Vision Video in 1989.
- The audio cassette *Faces, Mirrors, Masks: Twentieth Century Latin American Fiction* was released by National Public Radio in 1984.
- *Carlos Fuentes: An Interview in Spanish* was released on audio cassette by Ediciones del Norte in 1988.
- *Carlos Fuentes Reads from* Distant Relations was released on audio cassette by In Our Times Arts Media in 1986.

Pancho Villa

Pancho Villa was a real person in the Mexican revolution. In the book, he is presented as a showman who knows how to manipulate the American reporters who follow him. When the press asks about the person who was shot in the back by his people, Villa has the body of Bierce dug up out of his grave and shot again, from the front, so that the revolutionaries will not get a bad reputation. Then he has his soldiers kill Arroyo for embarrassing the revolution with the shooting of the old gringo.

Raul Walsh

Raul Walsh is the photographer traveling with Pancho Villa. Walsh is one of the novel's actual historical personalities: he was one of the pioneers of silent movies.

Harriet Winslow

A thirty-one-year-old woman from Washington, DC, Harriet lived with her mother and was engaged to marry a corporate lobbyist, Mr. Delaney, who idealized her and would not have sex with her until after they married. Her father had left to fight in the army in Cuba when Harriet was sixteen, and she never saw him again: for years, Harriet and her mother lived on the pension the government sent them because it was thought her father was killed in the war. However, Harriet knew from a letter he had sent that he actually had moved in with another woman.

An older Harriet moves to Mexico to become

the schoolteacher for the Miranda family. However, when she arrives, the wealthy family has abandoned their huge home and it has been taken over by Arroyo and his band of revolutionaries. Harriet decides to stay because she feels responsible for the Mirandas' house, having received a month's salary in advance from them. She also intends to teach American ways to the children of the revolutionaries. In Bierce, Harriet finds a substitute for the father who abandoned her, and in Arroyo, she finds the promise of romantic adventure, and also a sympathetic figure who understands what it is like to be rejected by one's father. Harriet explains to Bierce that her sexual relationship with Arroyo is only to keep him from taking the old gringo's life, although the satisfaction she feels during the experience is real and profound.

After Arroyo kills Bierce, Harriet returns to Washington and tells reporters that Arroyo shot down an officer in the American army. This news brings political pressure on the revolutionaries which results in Arroyo's death. Harriet also tells U.S. government officials that the old gringo was her father, who had actually survived the Cuban invasion and had come to Mexico to rescue her. Thus, Bierce is buried in her father's grave at Arlington National Cemetery. The novel begins and ends with Harriet as an old woman, sitting alone in her apartment in Washington, remembering the events of her trip to Mexico.

Themes

Identity

All three of the principal characters in this novel have mixed feelings of both love and hatred toward their fathers. When Ambrose Bierce, the old gringo, charges recklessly toward the guns of the Federal troops and is triumphant, his first words are "I have killed my father." He imagines himself, having grown older and increasingly bitter, as having "invented myself a new family, a family of my imagination, through my Club of Parenticides, the target of destruction." He has even lost his chance to identify with his own children because one son became an alcoholic and the other took his own life, mirroring Bierce's own cynical attitude.

Harriet Winslow's sense of herself is based on her idea of honor, which is both supported and offended by memories of her father. The official story that is accepted by the war department is that he died serving his country during the 1898 invasion of Cuba, and in his honor, the U.S. government has sent his pension checks to Harriet and her mother. Harriet's secret shame is that she knows her father did not die in battle but abandoned his family to live with a woman who, because she was a Negro, was considered to be from a lower social order in early twentieth-century America. In a way, Harriet's affair with the Mexican peasant

Tomás Arroyo is based on her identification with her father.

Arroyo's father would not acknowledge his illegitimate son's existence: Arroyo remembers an incident from when he was nine years old, when a trusted servant allowed him to hold the ring of keys that opened all of the doors of the house, and the father shouted at the servant to "take those keys from the brat." Arroyo's strong sense of self comes from the mysterious documents that he cannot read, which he counts on to establish his legitimate claim to the land. This situation puts him in the odd position of being a Mexican revolutionary who counts on the authority of the King of Spain to give him a sense of self. For Arroyo's followers, taking over the Miranda estate is a victory of the poor over the rich, but for him it represents an ascension to his rightful place in the world, as heir to his father's possessions.

Culture Clash

Ambrose Bierce goes to Mexico to die in this novel, because to him Mexico is a strange and dangerous frontier. He knows that it is a place where he can die fighting, and not just wallow away in corruption as he would in America. "Let me imagine for you a future of power, force, oppression, pride, indifference," Bierce tells General Arroyo. When the general relates these words to the fate of the revolution, Bierce makes another statement that applies equally to the country and to the man: "The only way you will escape corruption is to die young."

The novel presents the Mexican revolution as a product of uncorrupted society, probably the only place on the continent where hope is earned fairly. The Mexican establishment, represented by landowners like Miranda and the Federal troops that guard them, is well on its way to moral impurity. The height of corruption is represented by wealthy Americans, such as William Randolph Hearst, Leland Stanford, and Harriet's fiancé, Delaney, who is false to his business associates and false to himself about their relationship. The lower-class Mexicans, however, do not see the differences between the two countries as being about corruption and violence. To them, the United States represents the kind of wealth for which they can dare to hope. As Harriet leaves the peasant Inocencio Mansalvo, the novel explains, "she knew that he would always keep an eye on the long northern border of Mexico, because for Mexicans the only reason for war was always the gringos." One culture is violent and the other refined, one corrupt and the other pure: "what mattered was to live with Mexico in spite of progress and democracy," Harriet thinks at the end, "that each of us carries his Mexico and his United States within him, a dark and bloody frontier we dare cross only at night: that's what the old gringo had said."

Death

Death is not feared by the characters in *The Old Gringo*. The Mexicans who encounter Bierce early in the novel acknowledge the fact that he came to Mexico to die. In the novel, the gringo quotes the real Ambrose Bierce in explaining why he welcomes death on his trip: "To be a gringo in Mexico, ah, that is euthanasia." Going to Mexico is Bierce's way of putting himself out of his misery, of freeing himself from the complications of American life that he knows are false. He gains the respect of Arroyo's men by riding straight into enemy gunfire because the possibility of death does not frighten him. Arroyo himself is quite fearless, fully aware that success in the revolution would eventually make him as corrupt as the heartless, passionless men he is fighting to overthrow, like President Diaz, who, he points out, was once a revolutionary like himself.

Topics for Further Study

- Read Ambrose Bierce's famous short story "An Occurrence at Owl Creek Bridge," which is mentioned in this novel. What does that story tell you about the character of Bierce as Carlos Fuentes portrays him here?

- Pancho Villa's reputation is still controversial: many people see him as a hero of the revolution, while many others see him as a criminal who manipulated the media. Research his life story and explain whether you think he did more good or harm for the development of Mexico.

- Many Americans are familiar with songs that were popular in 1914, such as "St. Louis Blues" or "Peg O' My Heart." Research some Mexican music that was popular at the time, and compare it to popular music of Mexico today.

- How has the relationship between the United States and Mexico changed since the passage of the North American Free Trade Agreement in 1994? Do you think it will it help or hinder Mexican economic development? Explain what you think one of the three main characters of this novel (Bierce, Harriet, or Arroyo) would say about it and why.

Perhaps the most stirring symbol of death in this story is the open grave at Arlington National Cemetery that is waiting for the body of Harriet Winslow's father. According to one story, Major Winslow was a war hero who died serving his country, but another story holds that he lived out his life in a cheap apartment with his mistress. Either way, the same open grave awaits him. In the end, the grave is filled with the body of Ambrose Bierce, an exalted resting place for someone who went to Mexico to die in anonymity. Bierce states throughout the story that he wants to leave a good-looking corpse: having been shot, exhumed and shot again, his corpse is not in good physical shape, but it is given a hallowed resting place, while the corpse of Tomás Arroyo is put out in the desert to be forgotten.

Style

Structure

The action in *The Old Gringo* is structured within a framing device; that is, the main part of the novel is "framed" by scenes of Harriet Winslow described in the present tense, sitting in her apartment in Washington and reflecting on events long past. Periodically throughout the course of the novel this present-tense Harriet is mentioned briefly, reminding readers that the story being told is not being narrated directly but is a summary of one character's memories. Many novels use a framing device to contain their story within a particular context, but *The Old Gringo* has an even more complex structure: it presents a frame within a frame. The first and last settings are in Harriet's apartment, but the second and second-to-last actions happen after the death of the gringo, with the exhuming of his body coming in chapter two, and the story of how Arroyo was executed—which should come right after the exhumation chronologically—coming in the last chapters. This makes Harriet's final days in Mexico a frame that is in itself framed by her sitting in her apartment.

Symbolism

Fuentes writes in a way that makes the most of the objects with which his characters interact, raising them to a symbolic level beyond their role in the telling of the story. One example of this is the way that Arroyo talks about the worm in the bottle of tequila in chapter five: "The worm eats some things and you eat others. But if you eat things like I was in El Paso ... then the worm will attack you because you don't know him and he doesn't know you, Indiana General." Obviously, Arroyo's speech has greater significance than just a worm, which is drowned in liquor, and so readers are led to assume that his point about familiarity and different types of foods relates to Mexicans and Americans.

Fuentes's use of symbolism is not subtle, and should be clear even to those readers who do not approach novels as puzzles. The mirrors in the ballroom represent self-awareness: if this is not clear from Bierce's oft-repeated question, "Did you look at yourself in the mirrors when you entered the ballroom?," the point is hard to avoid when General Arroyo explains that he left the ballroom unburned so that his men could see themselves. Another object in the story that is too mysterious to have less-than-symbolic value is the packet of ancient documents that Arroyo handles with such tenderness. The reader is never told whether they actually give legitimacy to Arroyo's claim to land, though it is implied that they do not. The important thing is not their actual worth, but what they mean to Arroyo: they represent his social legitimacy, and he believes in the documents so much, even though he cannot read them, that he kills Bierce out of frustration when they are burned. One final obvious symbol is the "open grave" in Arlington National

Cemetery: of course, the cemetery would not leave a hole in the ground waiting for someone who disappeared, but the phrasing of this item reminds readers of the chasm, the empty void, waiting for everyone at death.

Oedipus Complex

The father of psychoanalysis, Sigmund Freud, coined the term "Oedipus complex." It refers to the ancient Greek myth of Oedipus, who was sent away as an infant and, running into his birth father years later, did not recognize him and killed him, later marrying the man's wife—Oedipus's mother. In psychiatry, the Oedipus complex refers to the unconscious desire that makes a person wish to eliminate the parent of his or her own gender and replace the missing parent. In this story, Bierce is the acknowledged father figure, and the feelings that both Harriet Winslow and Tomás Arroyo have for him are nearly textbook examples of the psychoanalytic design. Arroyo sees himself in sexual competition with Bierce for Harriet's love, and it is for psychological reasons that he ends up shooting Bierce, who could otherwise have been an asset to his revolutionary cause. Harriet is attracted to Bierce as a father, as indicated in her near-panic regarding his relationship with his own daughter: after asking twice about his daughter during their most intimate conversation, she nearly screams out, "And your daughter?," as the narrator explains, "with a stubborn, controlled coldness." In the end, she adopts Bierce as her father and has him entombed under her father's name for all time.

In addition to their father-son-daughter triangle, each of the main characters has a desire to replace lost fathers. Even the old man, Bierce, thinks often about how much he is like his father: "The gringo thought how ironic it was that he the son was traveling the same road his father had followed in 1847." Arroyo never manages to move his troops out of the hacienda where his father—who had been violently chased away—ignored him throughout his childhood. And Harriet spends much time musing on the probable sex life of her father and his probable mistress.

Historical Context

Before the Revolution

Long before the revolution, which serves as the context for this novel, Mexico was a country steeped in political turmoil. In the early sixteenth century, conquerors from Europe overcame the indigenous peoples who lived there, notably the Maya, Aztecs, Olmecs, and Toltecs. Spain ruled the country as a colony from 1535 to 1821, when revolutionary forces were able to gain independence, in part because Spain itself was occupied by France.

Independence was followed by a series of revolts, as the country struggled to establish a unified national identity. President Antonio Lopez de Santa Anna, elected in 1933, tried to bring the numerous provinces that made up the country under one central government, which raised the question of who controlled Texas, leading to the Mexican-American war of 1846 to 1848. America won the war, and, in turn, Texas, and the border between the two countries was established as the Rio Grande River (which the old gringo crosses at the beginning of the novel).

After the war, the balance of power in Mexico shifted several times. Estate owners, many of whom did not live near their lands but only reaped the benefits of them, struggled against the peasantry who worked the lands. Uprisings broke out at different times, in different parts of the country. The liberal Benito Pablo Juarez led the fight for a new constitution in 1858, which included such benefits for the citizenry as freedom of speech and the right to vote for all males. He was elected president in 1861, but he incurred the wrath of Spain, France, and Great Britain by refusing to pay interest on loans from them: those countries sent invading forces to Mexico, and as a result, Juarez and his cabinet fled into exile for several years, during which a conservative government favoring the land owners took power. Juarez returned to power in 1865.

In 1877, Porfirio Diaz was elected president, a post that he held, with one brief interruption, until he was ousted by the revolution in 1910. Diaz had been a soldier during the political turmoil and ran unsuccessfully for the presidency twice, in 1867 and 1871. He led military uprisings after each defeat. During Diaz's tenure, Mexico became an active participant in the world economy, but the peasantry were discontent, left unable to share in the wealth that was generated.

Compare & Contrast

- **1914:** The assassination of archduke Franz Ferdinand, heir to the Austrian throne, sets off a chain of political events that draws most of the countries of the world into the First World War.

1985: Many of the countries that had formerly been in the Austro-Hungarian empire before the start of World War I are members of the Soviet Union.

Today: After the Soviet Union's dissolution in 1991, some countries are struggling to cope with independence and establish their own identities.

- **1914:** Feminist Margaret Sanger is forced to leave the United States for England to avoid prosecution for printing her pamphlet, "Family Limitation," which dealt with the subject of birth control.

  1985: U.S. abortion rights, which were established by the Supreme Court in the 1973 decision in *Roe v. Wade*, constitute one of the most talked-about political issues. Candidates for national offices endure tremendous pressure to declare themselves supporters for either the "pro-life" or "pro-choice" sides of the debate.

  Today: Scientific advances, such as time-released implants and "morning-after" pills, have made birth control a commonplace concern in the United States.

- **1914:** President Victoriano Huerta of Mexico, who had come to power by having his predecessor murdered, is forced to leave the country for exile. One of the decisive elements in his leaving was a military occupation of Mexico's main seaport, Veracruz, by the U.S. Atlantic fleet.
  1985: The administration of President Ronald Reagan, opposed to the leftist government of Nicaragua, arranges illegal arms shipments to guerrilla revolutionaries.
  Today: The U.S. government's intervention into the affairs of other countries is severely limited by its own laws and by United Nations supervision.

The Mexican Revolution: 1910–1920

In 1910, the Republic of Mexico was actually run as a dictatorship under President Diaz's control. Diaz had brought stability to the country and helped build its economy early in his long presidency, but he and his followers became increasingly totalitarian as the years went by. In order to build up the country's infrastructure and to provide government contracts for his friends, Diaz had to raise money by turning over more and more land to foreign interests, taking it out of the control of poor Mexicans. In 1910, Francisco I. Madero led a successful revolution against Diaz, sending him into exile, and in 1911 Madero was elected president.

Madero, however, did not deliver the country back to the people, and he became unpopular by allowing corruption to fester. In 1913, one of his generals, Victoriano Huerta, a former Diaz supporter, led a counterrevolution, took control of the government, and had Madero killed. Although Madero had been unpopular, the people deeply resented his murder. Several branches of revolution broke out across the country. The governor of Coahuila, Venustiano Carranza, led one; Emaliano Zapata led the revolution in the southern state of Morelos; and in Chihuahua, the revolution was led by Francisco ("Pancho") Villa, who appears as a character in *The Old Gringo*. The American press portrayed the media-savvy Villa as a modern-day Robin Hood.

In July of 1914, with his own people and the international community opposing him, Huerta resigned and left the country. The capital was taken over by followers of Carranza. Soon, Carranza was at odds with the other leaders of the revolution; in 1915, his forces fought against Villa's, and by 1916, Villa had lost any official claim on the gov ernment and was leading a band of outlaws in making raids across the Texas border. President Woodrow

Wilson sent U.S. troops under the command of General John "Blackjack" Pershing into Mexico to capture Villa. A new constitution in 1917 established Carranza as the country's president, but he was ousted and murdered in 1920, replaced by a former ally, General Alvaro Obregon.

Critical Overview

The Old Gringo has remained one of Carlos Fuentes's most widely read novels, in part because of the star-studded Hollywood movie adaptation that followed shortly after its publication. Many of the early reviews of the book expressed admiration for the story and for Fuentes as an author and as a writer. At the same time, though, many reviewers held back their praise, unsure about the novel's cool style. Earl Shorris's review in *The New York Times Review of Books* showed deep respect for the issues that Fuentes touches upon in *The Old Gringo:* "It is the work of an integrated personality, the artist who contains and illuminates all of the times and cultures of a nation." Shorris had difficulty finding fault. "The only serious flaw for me is that the book may be too concise. I wished for details to more fully realize the characters, to limit them less by their symbolic roles."

Gloria Norris mentioned in her review of *The Old Gringo* in *America* that "Fuentes uses the approach of the poet rather than the novelist." She went on to praise his rendering of Washington, DC, over his descriptions of the Mexican settings, adding that, "surprisingly, his Mexican figures are more like statuesque figures in a mural, while Bierce and Harriet are given more depth." Neither of Norris's comments are negative, but they both touch upon the most frequent causes of discomfort among reviewers: that this novel about Mexico is too distant from both its characters and its country.

John Seabrook, writing for *The Nation*, said early in his review that "*The Old Gringo* is a fascinating novel to reflect on, though at times a dense, bewildering one to read." Like Norris, Seabrook was more impressed with Fuentes's handling of his American characters, feeling that the Mexican characters functioned as symbols, as explanations for the mind of modern Mexico, rather than as people. Thomas R. Edwards picked up on the same idea in his review. After explaining the symbolic positions of Arroyo, Winslow, and Bierce, he pointed out that their symbolic functions were sometimes too simplistic, that the author was trying too hard to convey ideas about sociology. "This triptych of characters risks being too obvious a device to show the distance between Mexican and American minds," Edwards wrote in *The New York Review of Books*, "but Fuentes sometimes forces the point he wants to make about them on the reader—there are a few too many remarks like 'each of us carries his Mexico and his United States within him' or 'be us and still be yourself' or 'I want to learn to live with Mexico. I don't want to save it.'"

Michiko Kakutani took an opposite view, explaining in *The New York Times* that Fuentes's cultural and racial myths actually bring life to the love triangle the novel is centered around, making it "as inevitable as it is real." One of the least forgiving reviews was written by noted novelist, poet, and playwright John Updike, for *The New Yorker*. Updike expressed admiration for what

Fuentes was trying to achieve, but even more pressing for him was his regret that, in his opinion, *The Old Gringo* is "a very stilted effort, static and wordy, a series of tableaux costumed in fustian and tinted a kind of sepia I had not thought commercially available since the passing of Stephen Vincent Benet." While other reviewers appreciated the novel's enchanting, heavily stylized tone, Updike could not accept the falseness of what is presented: he could not suspend his disbelief long enough to find much to admire in the book. "Fuentes is certainly intelligent," he concludes, "but his novel lacks intelligence in the sense of a speaking mind responsively interacting with recognizable particulars. Its dreamlike and betranced gaze, its brittle grotesquerie do not feel intrinsic or natural: its surrealism has not been earned by any concentration on the real."

What Do I Read Next?

- *Don Quixote*, the book that the old gringo says he intends to read some time, was written by Spanish novelist Miguel de Cervantes Saavedra and published in 1615. It is the classic story of idealism and of standing up to unbeatable odds.

- *The Complete Short Stories of Ambrose Bierce* is available in a 1985 paperback, edited by Ernest Jerome Hopkins. Among the most notable pieces referred to in Fuentes's novel are "A Horseman in the Sky," about a Union soldier who kills his father, a member of the Confederacy; and Bierce's most famous work, "An Occurrence at Owl Creek Bridge."

- Mexico's most honored contemporary poet was the late Nobel Prize laureate Octavio Paz. The most comprehensive volume of his work is 1987's *The Collected Poems of Octavio Paz 1957–1987*. This volume contains both English and Spanish versions of his poems.

- Most of Fuentes's novels received critical acclaim. Readers interested in his work may want to contrast the intellectualism of this book with the vigor of his first published novel, *Where the Air Is Clear* (1958).

- Carlos Fuentes is almost as well known for his essays as for his fiction. He frequently explores the character of his homeland. His 1996 collection *A New Time for Mexico* revisits themes explored in his book from twenty-five years earlier called *Tiempo mexicano* ("Mexican Time").

- Gabriel García Márquez is a Nobel Prize laureate from Columbia and one of Fuentes's contemporaries. His book *One Hundred Years of Solitude* (1969) is recognized as his masterpiece, and stylistically it resembles the work that Fuentes was doing in the 1960s. Like Fuentes, though, Marquez's style evolved, and his 1985 novel *Love in the Time of Cholera* is closer in style and tone to *The Old Gringo*.

- One of the most striking and influential novels by a Latin-American writer of Fuentes's generation was Argentine author Julio Cortazar's 1963 book *Hopscotch*, about international intrigue. Though the book's subject matter is not much like that of *The Old Gringo*, Cortazar's style is similar, and this book is widely praised as one of the best of the century.

- Reviewers have pointed out that British writer Malcolm Lowrey's 1947 novel *Under the Volcano* is one of the best examples of a non-Mexican capturing the country's essence. It is the fevered, nightmarish story of an English counsel's spiritual collapse.
- E. L. Doctorow's 1975 novel *Ragtime* shows the life of three American families in New York at roughly the same time as this story takes place. At the end of Doctorow's book, one of the characters runs away to join Pancho Villa and his bandits.

Sources

Thomas R. Edwards, "Pathos and Power," in *The New York Review of Books*, December 19, 1985.

Carlos Fuentes, *The Old Gringo*, translated by Margaret Sayers Peden, Farrar, Straus, 1985.

Michiko Kakutani, "The Old Gringo," in *The New York Times*, October 23, 1985, p. C21.

Gloria Norris, "The Old Gringo," in *America*, May 17, 1986, p. 416.

John Seabrook, "One of the Missing," in *The Nation*, January 18, 1986.

Earl Shorris, "To Write, to Fight, to Die," in *The New York Times Review of Books*, October 27, 1985, p. 1.

John Updike, "Latin Strategies," in *The New Yorker*, February 24, 1986, p. 98.

For Further Study

Alfonzo Gonzalez, *Carlos Fuentes: Life, Work and Criticism*, York Press, 1987.

> Written soon after the publication of *The Old Gringo*, this book is by an eminent researcher in Third-World studies.

Lanin Guyrko, "Twentieth-Century Literature," in *Mexican Literature: A History*, edited by David William Foster, University of Texas Press, 1994.

> Contains sections about various genres in different eras of Mexican history. A good reference source for putting Fuentes in an historical context.

Kristine Ibsen, *Author, Text and Reader in the Novels of Carlos Fuentes*, Peter Lang Publishing, 1996.

> Ibsen, the editor of a book about female authors in Mexico in the 1980s and 1990s, gives a detailed analysis of Fuentes's works and the ways in which they involve readers more than traditional fiction.

John Rutherford, *Mexican Society during the Revolution: A Literary Approach*, Oxford University Press, 1971.

> Examines the revolution and its leaders as they are depicted in literature written at the time.

Cynthia Steele, *Politics, Gender and the Mexican Novel, 1968–1989: Beyond the Pyramids*, University of Texas Press, 1992.

> Steele's work covers Fuentes's most active time as a novelist, and reviews the social attitudes that affected him and his contemporaries.

Maarten Van Delden, *Carlos Fuentes, Mexico and Modernity*, Vanderbilt University Press, 1997.

> Van Delden explores the schism between Fuentes's differing visions of Mexico.

Raymond Leslie Williams, *The Writings of Carlos Fuentes*, University of Texas Press, 1996.

> Focused principally on Fuentes's major novel *Terra Nostra*, this study examines the treatment of Mexican culture throughout the author's works.

Milton Keynes UK
Ingram Content Group UK Ltd.
UKHW032359120224
437723UK00012B/1047